# A PEEP
# AT EYPE

The dramatic events of 10th December 1881 brought Eype to the attention of the nation. These illustrations from *The Graphic* of 24th December 1881 show the moment when the balloon Saladin failed to land on Eype cliffs and was swept out to sea, carrying Walter Powell MP to his death.

# A PEEP
# AT EYPE

## THE STORY OF A DORSET
## VILLAGE IN POSTCARDS

Edited by
Paul Atterbury

EHG PUBLICATIONS
2002

# ACKNOWLEDGEMENTS

The postcards reproduced in this book have been drawn from a number of private collections in Dorset, and the publishers are very grateful for the advice, support and enthusiasm offered at all times by the owners of those collections. While a considerable number of Eype cards have been recorded, some are, inevitably, extremely rare.

Many residents of Eype, Symondsbury and Bridport have been generous with their knowledge, their records and their memories, and their contribution has been vital in the preparation of this book. Particular thanks are due to Chrissie Atterbury, Bill Bartlett, Roy Billen and family, Peter Cove, Sue and David Filsell, Danielle and Selwyn Holmes, Peggy Wrixton and Ruth Wrixton. Additional information was also supplied by Stephen Bartlett, Richard Barton, Martin Cox and Laurie Grimshaw. Details contained in the text have been drawn from the back numbers of various local and national newspapers and magazines, including *The Bridport News, The Dorsetshire, Devonshire & Somertsetshire Advertiser, The Daily Express, The Graphic* and *The Illustrated London News*. Also important in the preparation of the introduction was Barbara Kennett's *Eype* and *Its Church*, a booklet published by the author in 1966.

A number of the postcards reproduced in this book have been included with the permission of their publishers or the owners of their copyright, and particular thanks are due to:
The Francis Frith Collection, Salisbury, Wiltshire SP3 5QP. www.francisfrith.co.uk
Judges Postcards Ltd, St Leonard's-on-Sea, East Sussex TN38 8BN. www.judges.co.uk
Valentine images reproduced by kind permission of St Andrew's University Library from postcards published by James Valentine & Son, Dundee.
J. Salmon Ltd, Sevenoaks, Kent TN13 1BB
The publishers have used their best endeavours to trace the copyright holders of postcard images issued by photographers or publishers no longer in business.

A CIP catalogue record for this book is available from the British Library

First published in Great Britain in 2002 by the Eype Historical Group. Reprinted 2003.
Arden, Eype, Bridport, Dorset DT6 6AL
Printed and bound by Creeds, Broadoak, Bridport, Dorset DT6 5NL.

ISBN 0 9542881 0 6

*Front cover:* A detail from a famous postcard of Eype's main street, photographed in about 1900 and published by W. & E. Frost.
*Back cover:* Eype Beach in the 1990s. Reproduced courtesy of Michael J. Allen Photography, Delpool Picture Postcards, Poole, Dorset BH17 0RA.

## THE EYPE HISTORICAL GROUP

Founded in 2002 by a number of Eype residents, the Eype Historical Group has been established as a non-profit making organisation to study, research and record all aspects of the history of the village of Eype and its inhabitants, past and present.

A *Peep at Eype* is the Group's first publication. It is hoped that others will follow. The Group will be delighted to hear from anyone who has postcard images of Eype not included in this book, or any other photographs, documents, records or information relevant to the history of the village and its people.

A percentage of the income from the sales of this book will be used to support Eype village projects.

The Eype Historical Group, Arden, Eype, Bridport, Dorset DT6 6AL.
website: eypehistory.com

# EYPE'S POSTCARDS

Our fisheries are scant indeed,
Along the crescent sand;
But neighbours kind supply the need
Of epicures on land

The cliffs, with slopes and flats abound,
All facing the warm south;
And quietly you may lie down
In summer at Eype's mouth.

Here stands a 'chaumière' high and bold,
Where visitors take tea,
So nicely sheltered from the cold
By hedge and briar tree.

The sea is calm, the air is soft,
The beach is like a floor;
You fancy you could soar aloft,
While bathing near the shore.

There is no frost or chilly wet,
The place scarce knows such things;
The seasons there are summer heat
And pure delightful springs.

From *Symondsbury, A Poem*
by F. Bartlett, 1863.

Eype is a small coastal village between Bridport and Chideock in West Dorset, built largely around a lane that descends steeply towards the sea, and ending by an inlet in the cliffs formed by the mouth of the Eype stream. It is in the parish of Symondsbury, a far more substantial inland village listed in the Domesday Book. In the past the main activities in Eype were farming, fishing, boatbuilding and smuggling, but during the twentieth century tourism has become increasingly important. The development of tourism in Eype can be documented by postcards, for the history of the picture postcard seems to coincide precisely with Eype's emergence as a resort.

For so small a village, Eype has generated over the last century a remarkable quantity and variety of postcards. Well over 200 have been recorded, and practically every corner of the village has appeared in a postcard at one time or another. Certain views seem to have been perennially popular, with similar cards issued over the decades by a number of publishers. At the same time, there are many that are individual or even quirky in their choice of subject, and can only have had a very limited appeal. The cards depict all parts of the village, including the beach and its surroundings, general views, the main features of the village along the main road, including the pub and the hotel, Lower Eype and other outlying parts, the top of the village by the church, Higher Eype and Down House Farm and Cockcrowing, the junction of the lane with the old Bridport road. By postmark evidence, the earliest recorded card is 1903, but several of the early images can be dated from internal evidence to the late 1890s and may have been issued then. A number of cards predate the First World War, but a far greater number were issued in the 1920s and 1930s, reflecting the increased popularity of the village as a resort. The years following the Second World War witnessed another surge in card production, inspired in part by the development of the caravan and camp sites adjacent to the village. Since then, the number of cards being issued has steadily declined, to the point that hardly any specific Eype cards are now available.

Eype's popularity in postcard terms is also reflected by the number of publishers recorded. Many of the big names, Frith, Valentine, Tuck, Judge, Dixon, Salmon, Hinde have issued Eype views at one time or another. Frith alone have records of over sixty Eype postcards, ranging in date from the late 1890s to the 1960s. Equal numbers have been issued by local publishers, Claud Hider, Hine Brothers, W. & E. Frost, Potts, Hare Brothers, Chapman of Dawlish and Dearden & Wade of Bournemouth. Many cards, especially from the first decades of the twentieth century, are completely anonymous and so their photographers and publishers may never be identified. In any case, little enough is known about some of the postcard producers who can be named, many of whom were primarily photographers. It is a measure of the impact of local tourism that so many small-scale card publishers could be commercially successful over a considerable period. More surprisingly, there are even cards printed in France and Germany, and at least one is recorded issued by an American publisher.

# THE STORY OF EYPE

Eype's early history is intertwined with legend and romance. According to some authorities, the village was founded in the seventh century BC by wandering Greek traders who built a temple and burial place on Quarr Hill, to the north. They came from Epirus, hence the name Eype. By other accounts, they called their temple Hellas, a name perpetuated by Hell Lane and Hell Farm. Another source for the name is said to be Egypt, a reflection of the popular description over several centuries of wanderers, or gypsies, as Egyptians. Quarr Hill has gypsy associations. There is also some evidence of Roman occupation, in the form of a Romano-British sculpted head excavated in Duck's Bottom. Marauding Vikings also visited, and their legacy can be seen, it is said, in the propensity towards red hair in long-established village families, of which there are many. Of the fifty Symondsbury and Eype family names listed in the Hearth Tax returns for 1662-1664, ninety per cent were found to be still represented in the 1970s. Also long established, apparently, is the tradition of smuggling, for centuries a major enterprise for the farmers, fishermen and boatbuilders who formed Eype's population, and made entirely believable by the remoteness, even today, of the beach. Many are the tales of the battles of wits that took place between the Revenue men, and the cunning fishermen's wives whose voluminous skirts could easily conceal a cask or two when they were seated and busy net-making.

While Symondsbury is recorded in the Domesday Book, documentary records of Eype seem to start, according to Hutchin's *History of Dorset*, in the reign of Edward III, when a manor and a farm in the possession of John de Bares was recorded at Estieype-juxta-Symondesberghe, or Estyepe. This, one of a number of recorded spellings, may have come from the same root as the word steep. By the reign of Elizabeth I, it was held by Henry Molyns and in 1671 it was sold by Lady Francis, Dowager Duchess of Somerset to a group of local men including Sir John Strode of Parnham and John Hoskins of Beaminster. They in turn sold it to the Minson family, and it was subsequently divided into various ownerships. In 1865, for example, part was owned by the Rolle family of Bicton, Devon.

A few of Eype's houses, for example Ship's Lights and April Cottage, can de dated back to the late eighteenth century or early nineteenth century, but little is known in detail until the Victorian era. By then the village had grown considerably; the 1851 census revealed that 269 people were residents. Mr Bartlett's 1863 poem, an excerpt of which is quoted above, suggests that Eype was receiving visitors by that date, and there was a 'chaumière', or shelter to cater for their needs. During that century, two major events, in effect, put the village on the map. The first was the building of the church, which was consecrated on 25th August 1865. Despite its status as a chapel of ease, St Peter's is a grand and substantial building, described soon after it was completed as 'a handsome edifice in the Early Decorated style.' It was built as a memorial to a former rector, the Reverend Gregory Raymond, and funded by Raymond's bequest to the parish of £3,000. Talbot Bury was the architect, and local stone from Sloes Hill and Bothenhampton was used. Minton encaustic tiles, a range of stained glass windows, a font and pulpit in Bath stone and Purbeck marble carved by R. L. Boulton of Worcester, fine woodwork and a silver chalice, paten and flagon given in 1865 by John Pitfield made this an exceptional church for such a small village. To put its grandeur in context, a fully equipped village church could be built in the 1860s for under £1,000. The scale is dramatic, the setting high above the village is magnificent, and it has long served as a landmark and a beacon for sailors. The church may have brought more visitors to the village, its appeal underlined by the opening by Robert Warren of the Ship's Lights as a refreshment room in 1880.

The second event was the tragedy that befell the balloon Saladin on Saturday 10th December, 1881, an accident that resulted in the death of Walter Powell, MP for Malmesbury. The balloon, carrying Captain Templer of the Royal Engineers, Mr Powell and Mr Agg-Gardner, ascended at Bath at 1.55pm on a mission for the Meteorological Office. At high altitude it flew southwards over Wells, Glastonbury, Langport, Crewkerne and Beaminster, carried along by a rising wind. Over Symondsbury, they came down to about 100 feet, and decided to find a landing place. What happened next was described by Captain Templer in his Official Report: 'To avoid the little village of Eype, Mr Powell threw out some ballast... I opened the valve and we descended about 150 yards short of the cliff. The balloon on touching the ground dragged a few feet, and I rolled out of the car with the valve line in my hand. This caused the balloon to ascend about eight feet, when Mr Gardner dropped off, and unfortunately broke his leg. I called to Mr Powell, who was standing in the car, to come down the line. He took hold of the line, and in a few seconds the line was torn through my hands. The balloon rose rapidly. Mr Powell waved his hand to me and I took his compass bearing.' The balloon was swept out to sea and soon disappeared from view and, despite extensive searches by local fishing boats, steam tugs and naval vessels over the next few days, no trace of it, or Mr Powell was found. Two villagers, David Forsey and Robert Warren, witnessed the accident and rushed to give assistance. Helped by other villagers, William Harvey, Frederick Hussey and William Tuck, they carried Mr Gardner to the New Inn, where he was treated by a doctor from Bridport while Captain Templer set off to organise searches. Both Forsey and Warren gave graphic accounts to local journalists, with Forsey's being quoted entirely in the Dorset vernacular.

The Saladin disaster received extensive coverage in both local and national newspapers and interest was maintained over the Christmas period, encouraged by lengthy and well illustrated reports in both *The Graphic* and *The Illustrated London News* on 24th December. As a result, many people came to Eype to visit the site of the accident. There were a number of reported sightings of the balloon, from the Channel Islands, France and Northern Spain, but all proved to be groundless. On 31st December a barometer case from the balloon was washed up on Chesil Beach, but nothing else was ever found at the time, and by 23rd December Mr Powell had been presumed dead, and the names of candidates selected to fight the election for his seat had been announced. Some years later the remains of the balloon were found in the Pyrenees, but, again, without any trace of Mr Powell.

During the late Victorian and Edwardian periods Eype became increasingly well-known as a quiet resort, with holiday-makers drawn there by the beach and the fishing. The proliferation of postcards is a measure of the village's new popularity at this time. Camping on the beach and the undercliff became popular from about 1903, a tradition started by masters and boys from Sherborne School. The first chalets were built in the fields by the cliffs, initially temporary wooden structures but becoming gradually more permanent. This pattern was maintained up to the First World War, and continued in a similar vein after the war. Eype played little part in the war itself, but a number of residents answered the call. In January 1915 the Howe Battalion of the 2nd Royal Naval Brigade was billeted in Bridport and over the next few weeks a complex network of practice trenches was dug over Eype Down. In February 1915 the Battalion left the area, and later that year took part in the Gallipoli landings.

Eype was next in the news in 1923. In August of that year a major cliff fall narrowly missed a

*Eype Beach showing Thorncombe Beacon, Bridport.* Publisher unknown. Postmark unclear but probably 1905. This early hand-coloured card shows the cliffs and the beach before the building of the hut on Fisherman's Green and the chalet in the Sevenlawns field.

*Eype Beach and Thorncombe Beacon.* Publisher unknown. Unused, 1930s. This hand-coloured card shows the fishermen's hut, the Whetham family's completed chalet, and some of the first small chalets, White Hut and Isle View, in the adjacent field. Also notable is the erosion of the cliffs, with much of the wall around the Sevenlawns field gone.

*Eype Beach*. Published by Dearden & Wade, Bournemouth, no.1965. Postmarked 1963. The cars have arrived and parking in the Sevenlawns field is well established. Although this card was issued in the 1960s, the cars suggest an earlier date for the photograph.

*Greetings from Eype's Mouth*. Published by Frith's, no. EPE 58. Postmarked 1961. Composite cards of this type became popular from the 1950s. Details that help to date the images include the Fort Bungalow still standing below the Bonville Hotel, now the Eype's Mouth Hotel, and Sunita, the early name for Eype House Caravan Park.

party picnicking on the beach, but destroyed their kettle sizzling at the base of the cliffs. A rather more significant event had happened the previous June when, in an article headed 'The Glories of West Dorset', the *Daily Express* had announced that Eype was the winner in a competition among the readers to find the quietest holiday resort in the country. Major Jourdain, who selected Eype, wrote 'A straggling line of cottages, and then a deep lane rioting with flowers leads to the beach, a tinkling stream accompanying you until it loses itself in mother ocean'. A special correspondent for the *Express* was despatched to Eype and he reported as follows: 'Any man who enters the quietest holiday place in England by motor-car commits the greatest sacrilege. One must tip-toe into paradise. I left my motor-car and, wondering whether I should not take off my shoes in such a fairyland, made my way among thatched cottages set like islands in a sea of honeysuckle and roses. Eype does not live in minutes and days and years. Flippant people there reckon time in generations; wiser ones think in centuries. I sat down on Fisherman's Green, a headland bluff, while Charlie Warren and Dick Warren, mere lads of fifty or so, told me of the good old times when dad's great-grandfather used to sit on that same green watching for the mackerel... At our feet stretched miles of fine sand. There is no post office at Eype. Certainly you may put a letter in a hole in the wall, and thus establish written communication with the outside world, but why write? The man who invented writing never came from Eype, which scorns such nonsense... There is one shop in Eype, with a shop window two feet square. I have qualms about mentioning it; somehow having a shop at all seems like letting Eype down, but it is not really as bad as that, because the visitor only discovers that there is a shop by accident. I took a great fancy to old Tom Forsey, the village boatbuilder. This splendid white-bearded ancient was building exactly as he has been building for the last sixty years... Old Tom sat on a clump of timber, saw in hand, and told of the old smuggling days. "Lookee yer" he whispered, "See the Inn there? Best zider in Dorset they sell there." I tiptoed gently up the hill and away through the Dorset lanes.'

During the 1930s Eype enjoyed a different kind of reputation, thanks to writers, artists and actors who came to stay at the Bonville Hotel, drawn to the area by local celebrities such as the playwright R. C. Sherriff. Tea and dinner dances, tennis tournaments and smart company brought modernity and urban sophistication to a village whose fame was based more on tranquility and traditional family holidays. The outbreak of the Second World War brought all this to an end, and Eype's beach became, like much of the coastline of southern Britain, a defended and inaccessible area. Concrete 'dragon's teeth' tank traps were spread across the beach, and barbed wire along the cliffs. A pillbox, built to defend the narrow estuary of the Eype stream, can still be seen today. Younger residents were called up, and the older ones formed themselves into the Home Guard. Four villagers died on active service, including, unusually, a father and son, Henry and Robert Sprake. The war did not affect the village directly, but there are plenty of memories of the great air battles that took place over Portland. The most significant event was the use of the Bridport, West Bay and Eype area for Operation Yukon on 11th June 1942, the rehearsal for the ill-fated combined operations raid on Dieppe the following August.

With the return of peace, Eype returned to its pre-war way of life as a quiet little resort offering the traditional pleasures of the old-fashioned seaside family holiday. With cars increasingly a fact of modern life, the village became more accessible to visitors. Camp sites, caravan parks and holiday chalets, or bungalets as they were called at the time, were developed in and around the village, becoming an important part of the village economy in a culture devoted more and more to the pursuit of leisure. Fishing as a way of life gradually disappeared, along with boatbuilding, and local residents had to look further afield for their means of employment. For the first time, property in Eype became attractive to visitors seeking weekend cottages or second homes. However, despite the many pressures for change, Eype has, remarkably, remained much the same. In the 1960s the Dorset Year Book described it as: 'A gem of all the fairest Dorset has to offer, concentrated in one spot. Peaceful, and with all the purposeful quiet of nature and all the unchanging strength of the encircling hills and downs; even in the pounding of the restless sea upon the beach at no great distance, sounding no more than a drowsy murmur, there is peace... Heaven's benediction on a haven of rest.'

# USING THIS BOOK

The cards illustrated are organised geographically, starting on the beach at the far southern end of the village, and then progressing up through the village to the church and Higher Eype. When a selection of similar views are shown, these are arranged in date order. Anyone wishing to identify the locations can do so by exploring the village itself, and by finding the viewpoints from the surrounding footpaths. Most are still easily accessible and, remarkably, in many cases little has changed. To simplify this process, an outline map has been included.

Postmark dates are given when known, even though these are only helpful up to a point. Photographs used for the cards are obviously earlier than the postmarks, and many cards remained in use over long periods. Interestingly, many of the cards in the various private collections consulted are unused. This suggests that the postcard was more important as a souvenir than as a means of communication. Unused cards have been dated by internal evidence, and by comparison with other cards by the same publisher. The Eype Historical Group would, naturally, be delighted to hear about cards showing views of Eype not included in this book.

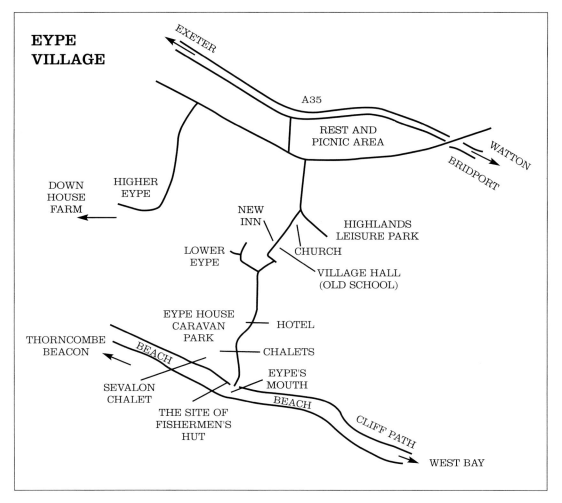

*Eype Village*. Published by W. & E. Frost, Bridport. Postmarked 1910. This early view of Eype, photographed in about 1899, was a popular image, with similar cards in monochrome and with hand-colouring issued by several publishers.

*Eype Village near Bridport*. Published by O. F. Stengel, London. Postmarked 1909. Versions of this popular view up the main street were issued by a number of publishers before and just after the First World War, in monochrome and with hand-colouring.

*The Post Office, Eype.* Published by Frith's, no. EPE 38. Unused 1950s. This colourful view shows Lower Eype looking towards Duck's Bottom, with Journey's End and Vine Cottage, at that point the Post Office, on the right.

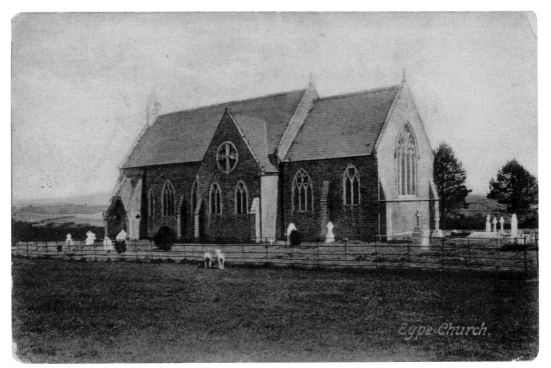

*Eype Church.* Published by W. & E. Frost. Postmarked 14 April 1915, and sent from Chideock to Wimbledon.

*Moonlight, Eype*. Publisher unknown, but labelled Real Photo Post Card, no. B38. Unused, pre-1914. This unusually romantic view, taken at the far western end of Eype beach, expresses the long-established appeal of the village as a special kind of resort. Other recorded views of this kind include one showing the pleasure steamer, the SS Victoria, passing Eype beach.

*Eype*. Published by Claud R. Hider, South Street, Bridport, no. 74. Unused, 1920s. This view of the estuary of the little Eype stream includes a rowing boat owned by Freddie Andrews, who lived at Whin Bridge from the early 1920s.

A JUNE AFTERNOON ON THE SANDS, EYPE.

*A June Afternoon on the Sands, Eype.* Publisher unknown. Unused, pre-1914. The nature of Eype Beach is constantly changing. It is usually composed of shifting pebbles and shingle, varying continuously, and unpredictably, in size. There is usually some sand at the western end, towards Thorncombe, but every now and then the entire beach becomes sandy, as this card indicates. Cards suggest that the sand was more common in the early part of the twentieth century. Throughout 2000 the beach was largely sand, but little has been seen since, except at low tide.

*Eype's Mouth*. Published by Hine & Sons, Bridport (also issued by Frith's, no.83372). Unused, pre-1914. This area above the beach was known as Fisherman's Green, traditionally used as a lookout for schools of mackerel. The hut, used by fishermen for shelter and for storing tackle and nets, was originally erected by Miss James of Wayside, the house behind the New Inn, a village benefactor who was also responsible for the renovation in 1904 of the old school as a new Reading Room. The boats were owned by the Warren family. The hut was used continuously until 1940 when it was removed by the army.

*Eype Cliffs*. Published by Frith's, no.65075. Postmarked 15 September 1915 and sent to Yeovil with the message: 'I am just off prawning are you coming?' This view shows the well-established habit of erecting tents and temporary structures on the cliffs and the beach. Potatoes were also planted on the undercliff and Eype was known for its 'earlies' grown there by Ern Neal.

*Eype Cliffs, Bridport.* Publisher unknown. Postmarked 22 June 1910, and sent as a birthday card to South Kensington, London. The habit of camping on the beach and the cliffs was apparently started in about 1903 by masters from Sherborne School bringing groups of boys for adventure holidays. This early view of a well-established and durable campsite may show one of these holidays.

*Bachelors Paradise.* Published by Hare Photos, Bridport. Unused, pre-1914. Following the inspiration of Baden-Powell, these young men probably came to Eype to enjoy fossil-hunting, fishing and other outdoor pursuits while camping on the undercliff. The figure on the right with the cap is Charlie Warren, a local fisherman who appears in other cards.

*Bridport, Eype Cliffs.* Published by W.& E. Frost, no.40088. Postmarked 12 April 1921 and sent to Belgium by a visitor staying at the Visitation Convent, Bridport. She wrote: 'Eype is a point of the sea… quite different from the Belgian coast.' This card, popular through the 1920s, shows the western end of the beach at low tide, and the typical scattering of large rocks. It was issued in both sepia and with hand-colouring.

*Eype Beach, near Bridport.* Published by James Valentine & Sons, Dundee. Postmarked 11 May 1906. The wheel trails on the beach were made by a small putt, or cart, used for collecting sand and gravel. If the sand weighed more than half a ton, two horses were needed to pull it.

*Eype Cliffs, Bridport.* Published by Hine Brothers, Bridport. Postmarked 15 August 1908, and sent to Loughton. The message actually includes the phrase: 'Wish you were here!'

*Eype Cliffs.* Publisher unknown. Postmarked 17 July 1907, sent to Mrs Buckman in Thame by her 'affectionate daughter,' who wrote: 'Mr Perrin has gone off fishing. They were up at 4 o'clock and we had mackerel for breakfast.' The cart trails are well defined, indicating a regular traffic in sand and gravel for building. Apart from the horse-drawn carts, there were donkeys with panniers. The field behind the stone wall was known as Sevenlawns and was owned by the Whethams. It was used by Will Warren for chicken rearing, and the chicken huts can be seen behind the wall.

*Eype Bridport.* Published by Hare Photos, Bridport. Unused, pre-1914. This card reveals much about the development of Eype. The beach is crowded with visitors and the hut on Fisherman's Green is newly erected. Also new is the enclosed hut on the far right. Mr Warren's chicken huts are still present but more important is the pile of building materials in the field. This is the start of the chalet known as Sevelons (named perhaps after the field, Sevenlawns). It was built in about 1911 for Austen Whetham, who owned the field.

*The Beach, Eype.* Published by H. Roy Knight, Caterer, West Bay, and printed in France. Unused, pre-1914. The Whetham's bungalow is complete, with its surrounding fence. Later, in 1938 the Whetham's sold the bungalow to Dorothy Carritt, it was sold again in 1951, and then again in 1962 to the present owner Mrs Wingfield Digby.

*Eype, Bridport.* Published by Hine & Sons, Bridport. Unused, pre-1920. The boats drawn up, and the tackle around the hut indicate the amount of fishing regularly carried out from the beach for lobsters, prawns and particularly for mackerel. When mackerel shoals were spotted, the boats worked in pairs, with a seine net between them, driving the fish towards the beach.

*Eype, Bridport.* Publisher unknown, but labelled Real Photo Post Card, no.19. Unused, 1920s. The chalet to the far right was the first to be erected in the field owned by Thomas Lee, a local farmer and dairyman. It had a distinctive green roof and was called, appropriately, Green Roofs.

*Eype Beach.* Published by Claud R. Hider, South Street, Bridport, no. 440. Unused, 1920s. By the time this photograph was taken, with its posed groups, Eype had become a popular resort. Similar views are found on a variety of cards with postmarks through the 1920s and 1930s.

*The Beach, Eype.* Published by Potts, Bridport. Postmarked 19 August 1930 and sent to Twickenham with the message: 'Had a comfy journey down and doing ourselves very well.'

*Eype.* Published by Hare Photos, Bridport. Postmarked 24 July 1914 and sent to Essex. The message is unusual: 'We saw a polo match last night held in the harbour (West Bay, presumably). Bridport lost 4-2. Round the other side of the cliffs is where Ernie and I got cut off by the tide. You need not swank with your camera, for we have had our photo taken looking awfully brown, haven't any skin on my nose.' Ten days after this card was sent, Britain was at war with Germany.

*Eype Beach, Teatime.* Publisher unknown. Unused, mid 1920s. The rocky and generally sandy western end of the beach is still a popular site for picnics.

*Eype.* Published by Potts, Bridport. Unused,1920s. The foreground underlines the point that cliff erosion is continuous, and generally gradual.

G.6864

EYPE CLIFFS NEAR BRIDPORT

*Eype Cliffs near Bridport.* Published by James Valentine & Sons, Dundee, no.G6864. Unused, 1930s. Dramatic erosion of the cliffs has brought the Sevelons chalet steadily closer to the cliff edge. Today, the chalet is only a few yards from the edge. However, there have been major falls between Eype and West Bay, notably ones in 1902 and 1923 that were reported by the local press. The undercliff and inlet between Eype's Mouth and West Bay was known as Clay Knapp, the site of a major landslip in September 1902, when a party walking along the beach had a narrow escape, as reported in the *Bridport News*: 'One piece, weighing some hundredweights, rolled down amongst the party, passing so near to Miss Read that it caught her umbrella and turned it into a shapeless object. The piece also hit Mr Knight who was knocked some distance. He was much bruised and shaken and lost his hat.'

25

*Eype Beach, Bridport.* Published in the West Dorset Series, no.339. Unused, late 1930s. Despite the complete lack of sand, the popularity of the beach continues, with plenty of visitors braving the sea.

*Eype Beach near Bridport.* Published by Dearden & Wade, Bournemouth, Sunny South Series. Unused, 1960s. Issued in monochrome and colour, and in other, similar versions. With cars much in evidence, the Sevenlawns field has been given over to parking. The first cars came in the 1920s and some early visitors drove their cars down the track onto the beach. Getting back up was a different matter and frequently help was required from the fishermen and horses. By now the fishermen's hut has disappeared, along with Fisherman's Green and much of the wall, the latter the result of erosion.

*Eype's Mouth.* Published by Chapman & Son, Dawlish, no.24385. Unused, 1950s. This postwar view shows many changes. The double-doored stone hut on the left was built during the war as an ammunition store. More chalets have appeared in the Lee field. To the right is the caravan park, known then as Sunita, established by the Harleys who had bought Eype House, built 1896, from the Hughes family.

*Eype.* Published by Judges Ltd. Unused, 1950s. The boats indicate that fishing is still going on. Sevelons has been painted to give it a half-timbered look. At the bottom of the steps there used to be a small wooden hut where Mr and Mrs Payne sold refreshments.

*Eype's Mouth*. Published by Chapman & Sons, Dawlish, no.24859. Unused, 1950s. This card offers a clearer view of the chalets and the Eype House caravan park, with Higher Eype in the distance. The dark chalet in the centre was owned by the Walker family of Four Foot Farm. In the centre foreground can be seen a fortified pill box, part of the invasion defences built in 1940. It still survives.

*The Cliffs. Eype's Mouth* Published by Frith's, no. EPE 7. Unused, 1950s. This offers a fine view of the downs and Thorncombe, with Golden Cap and Lyme Regis in the distance

*Untitled*. Published by PlastiChrome, USA. Unused, 1960s. This coloured card shows the steps to the beach, built just before the war, and the fishing tackle box above the steps installed by Jim Bartlett.

THE CLIFFS AND BEACH, EYPE'S MOUTH

*The Cliffs and Beach, Eype's Mouth*. Published by J Salmon Ltd, Sevenoaks. Unused, mid 1970s. This modern, coloured card shows a typically busy, early summer weekend at Eype beach.

*Boat Rest, Eype's Mouth*. Published by Frith's, no.EPE.30. Unused, 1960s. Known as the gully, this was a traditional resting place for boats, high above the tide line. The two in the centre, built by Tom Forsey, the village boat-builder, and showing his typical 'broad in the beam' style, were owned by Freddie Andrews and Frankie Fry. Today, a few small boats still remain drawn up by the mouth of the Eype stream.

*Thorncombe Beacon, Eype*. Published in the West Dorset Series, no.52. Unused, late 1930s. Taken from the cliff path on the descent towards Seatown, this shows the magnificent view eastwards from Thorncombe along the Dorset coast towards Chesil Beach and Portland.

*Eype Beach*. Published by Claud R. Hider, South Street, Bridport, no. 441. Unused, 1920s. This is an unusual view of the beach from the cliffs above the rocky western end, with West Bay in the distance.

*Eype Cliffs, Bridport*. Publisher unknown. Unused, dated in pencil 1919. This early view from the cliffs to the west shows the Whetham chalet with its surrounding fence, the smaller cliff edge enclosure and a surviving chicken hut by the wall. On the beach a tent and the well-defined tracks of the sand and gravel carts can be seen.

*Eype Cliffs, Bridport.* Published by Hine Brothers, East Street Library, Bridport. Postmarked 27 September 1921, and sent by Mr Miles, a bootmaker from Basingstoke, to his son.

*Eype.* Published by Potts. Unused, 1920s. Tents on the beach and the first chalet in the Lee field reflect Eype's increasing popularity.

*Eype, Bridport.* Published in the West Dorset Series, no.334. Unposted, but carries an Edward VIII stamp, thus 1936. This view from the west shows Eype House, a chalet and a gypsy caravan in the Lee field, and Sevelons now without its fence. Portland can be seen in the far distance.

*Eype Downs, Bridport.* Published by Gyngell & Shephard, Bridport. Unused, 1920s. Looking north towards Somerset, this card shows what is still one of Eype's best views.

178 Eype, Bridport

*Eype, Bridport.* Publisher unknown, no.178. Unused, 1920s. Another unusual view from the west, this card shows Fisherman's Green, with one of the old chicken huts and the temporary ladder down to the beach by the already crumbling end of the wall. Virtually all the foreground shown in this card has since disappeared through erosion.

*Eype. The Beach* Published by Judges Ltd. Unused, late 1950s. Piled up behind the boats are the ' dragon's teeth', concrete tank traps installed on the beach in 1940 as part of the invasion defences, and still surviving today.

*Eype.* Publisher unknown, no.53. Unused, 1930s. This unusual view looking eastwards along the beach includes fishing boats, holiday campers enjoying the sun outside their tents and Clay Knapp, with the landslip of 1902. Spoil from the construction of the esplanade at West Bay was dumped here to build up the cliffs.

*Eype from East Cliff.* Published by Valentine & Sons, Dundee, no. H.839. Unused, 1930s. Taken from the cliff path that climbs towards West Bay, this shows Whin Bridge to the left, the Bonville Hotel and Four Foot House, with Higher Eype and the Downs in the background.

*Eype and Cliff from the Downs.* Published by Raphael Tuck & Sons, London, no.Eype 9. Postmarked 18 (month unclear) 1939. Taken from Higher Eype, this view shows the village and the hotel with the cliff-top fields rolling away to the east. In the centre foreground there is a fine hay rick, made by Ern Neal, a champion rickmaker, thatcher and hedger. During the war the ricks were used for bayonet practice.

*Eype Village.* Published by Hine Brothers, Bridport. Postmarked 6 August 1904, and sent from a Miss West to her niece in Norfolk. The message says: 'Auntie has a bathe every morning-she wishes she had little Margery with her then the waves could go over both !' Issued in both monochrome and hand-coloured versions, this is the most popular Eype postcard and variants showing this view were on sale at least until the 1960s. The viewpoint, with the gateway in the hedge, is still much the same today. Even the gateposts are the same. It is possible to date this photograph to about 1898. Much the same image was later issued in the W. & E. Frost Series and by Frith's, no.43872, and many examples are known with pre-1914 postmarks.

*Bridport, Eype Village.* Published in the W.& E. Frost Series. Postmarked 27 March 1910. These two cards show how the same photograph, with minor differences, was issued by different publishers.

*Eype*. Published by Claud R. Hider, South Street, Bridport, no.71. Unused, 1920s. Visible in the centre is the terrace of four houses known as Balloon Cottages, named after the Saladin balloon accident of 1881. Later, Jack Bendin bought the cottages and Goldenacre Field in front of them, and two were demolished. The remaining two were renamed Pilgrim's Latch and Pilgrim's Rest.

*Eype*. Published by Potts, Bridport. Unused, 1920s. To the right of the centre are Arthur Day's sheds that used to stand at the far end of the Whin Bridge field, used as a piggery.

*A General View of Eype.* Published by Raphael Tuck & Sons, London, no. Eype 1. Unused, 1920s. The chalet in the field to the left of centre was known as Croft-an-Righ. Another version of this card was sent by someone staying in this chalet to a friend in the Isle of Wight.

*Eype Village, near Bridport.* Published by Valentine & Sons, Dundee, in their Silveresque series. Unused, late 1930s.

EYPE. BRIDPORT

*Eype, Bridport.* Publisher unknown. Postmarked 31 August 1948 and sent from Vine Cottage to a Miss Reece in Aldershot. The message says: 'tomorrow we are going to Portland to see HMS Vanguard.' The gate, shown in so many views, was known locally as the 'courting gate'.

EPE.3. EYPE VILLAGE

*Eype Village.* Published by Frith's, no. EPE 3. Unused, 1950s. With Four Foot House and the hotel in the foreground, this view looks north towards Higher Eype. Greystones, the house at the right end of Higher Eype, was built in 1939 by the playwright R. C. Sherriff, who wrote *Journey's End*.

*Good Luck from Eype*. Published by Valentine & Sons, Dundee, in their Silveresque series. Postmarked 4 July 1941 and sent to Mr and Mrs Linsdell of Merton, South London. This card, the earliest of the composite type, continued to be issued in similar versions by Valentine's at least until the late 1950s. Eype was not easily accessible during the Second World War as the beach and cliffs were restricted zones closed to the public.

*Eype*. Published by Judges Ltd. Postmarked 21 June 1963 and sent to Tewkesbury. The message is simply: 'Regards'

*Greetings from Eype*.Published by Chapman & Sons, Dawlish. Postmarked 29 July 1963 and sent to Salisbury.

*Eype, Ship's Lights*. Published by Judges Ltd. Postmarked 24 August 1965 and sent to London. Built by the Warren family and owned by them over many decades, this house was originally known first as The Cottage then later became Star Cottage because of the star-shaped window in the front door. It was used as a tea shop at least from 1880 to 2000.

*Cottage at Eype*. Published by Frith's. Postmarked 15 October 1903. This shows Mrs Edith Warren standing in the doorway of her cottage, a general store selling groceries, sweets and fishing tackle. Later, this became a teashop known as Ship's Lights. The cottage was built by her husband's grandfather. Mrs Warren lived in it all her married life and, according to her obituary, printed on 24 January 1902, she 'over a period of 42 years… never spent a night out of it… and had never been to any public entertainment in her life.' By contrast Mr Warren was a sailor and visited many parts of the world.

*Eype*. Published by R.D.Barrett, South Street, Bridport. Postmarked August 1906. The notice above the door offers 'Hot Water', for visitors having a picnic on the beach.

*Eype*. Published by Claud R.Hider, South Street, Bridport, no.330. Unused, 1930s. Port Cottage, adjacent to the Warren's cottage, may have been owned by the Whetham family. After several changes of ownership, it has recently been extended. The arched gateway into the garden survived until the early 1990s. Mrs Warren's son Charles, who died in 1950, can be seen behind the 'honey cart' which was used for the collection and disposal of sewage.

A *Peep at Eype*. Published by Potts, Bridport. Unused, 1930s. Another view of Port Cottage, then owned by Mrs Chinnery, with Charles Warren in the foreground. It was so named because of the porthole-shaped window in the front door. There seems to be a good crop of potatoes, perhaps 'Eype Earlies', in the garden.

*Puffer Bungalow, Eype.* Published by Claud R.Hider, South Street, Bridport, no.763. Unused, 1930s. The card shows on the far left Arthur Day's shed and boathouse that stood in the Whin Bridge field, in the centre Whitelands, then a bungalow recently built by George Bonfield, and on the right, the Puffer (or Puffa) cottage formed from two former Great Western Railway carriages. These were demolished in the 1960s and a new house was built on the site, Hookery Nook. Whitelands survives, much enlarged.

*Untitled.* Publisher unknown. Unused, 1930s. In the early 1920s Freddie Andrews and his new wife Daisy built themselves a cottage in the Whin Bridge field, formed from a retired Great Western Railway carriage of 1903 and two attached sheds, one of which was a rescued beach hut. Freddie and Daisy had one daughter and the cottage remained in the Andrews family until 1987, shortly after Daisy's death. The cottage survives, much loved by its present owners, and well known locally. Over the years it has been painted a number of colours, including green and maroon, and is now in Great Western chocolate and cream.

*The Hotel, Eype.* Published by Raphael Tuck & Sons, London. Unused, 1930s. This pre-war view of the Bonville Hotel shows the tennis courts. At that time Eype was enjoying one of its periods of fashionable prosperity, and a number of famous names stayed in the hotel. Others were drawn by the popular Tea and Dinner Dances. In front of the hotel is Fort Bungalow, so named because of the cannon and shells over the front door. This concrete building, lived in by Cy Sprake at this time, was later demolished and replaced in the 1960s by a much larger house, Bonrosa.

*Bonville Hotel Eype.* Published by Chapman & Sons, Dawlish, no. 24484. Unused, 1950s. The Bonville Hotel, now Eype's Mouth Hotel, was originally built as three identical houses by George Bonfield, one of which he lived in himself. Later, a centre section, clearly visible in this card, was added to join two of the houses together. The tennis court has gone and a conservatory has replaced the garden steps.

*Seascape Bungalets Eype* Advertising card, based on a Frith's photograph, early 1960s. Built in 1959, this bungalet development, in the centre of the card to the right of the hotel, reflected Eype's growing importance as a family resort from the 1950s. Facilities included a shop, a games room and a TV room. Now known as Golden Acre Chalets, this holiday development has, over the decades, brought thousands of visitors to Eype.

*Untitled.* Published by Frith's. Unused, early 1960s. The shop at Seascape Bungalets.

*Untitled.* Published by Frith's, no. E54063. Unused, early 1960s. This view shows the Seascape Bungalets soon after their completion.

*Providence Cottage Guest House. Eype.* Published by Chapman & Sons, Dawlish, no. 25309. Postmarked 7 September 1960. Included here because it offered accommodation in the Eype area, Providence Cottage is actually near Watton, at the top of Skilling Hill between Eype and Bridport.

*Eype* Published by Judges Ltd, no. 29004. Unused, 1960s. Now known as Pilgrim's Latch, this house was formed from two of the original terrace of four Balloon Cottages. This is built of cobb (a mixture of mud and straw rammed into a wooden frame that is removed when the material has hardened), a traditional west country technique, but more commonly associated with Devon.

*Eype Bridport* Published in the Arco Series. Postmarked 8 July 1923. This is an early version of a popular Eype view, looking down towards Lower Eype and Duck's Bottom, with Primrose Cottages on the left and Journey's End on the right in the distance. The timber on the right belonged to Tom Forsey, the boatbuilder, whose workshop was off the card to the left. He lived at No.1 Primrose Cottages.

*Eype* Published by Potts. Unused, 1920s. Duck's Bottom, with Journey's End and Vine Cottage on the right.

*The Valley, Eype.* Published by Raphael Tuck & Sons, London. Postmarked 17 August 1937. This view down towards Duck's Bottom shows the recently completed Sunnyside chalet bungalow, built in the orchard on the site of a garden shed. Eype Down in the distance is still bare of trees. The trees visible in the card below were planted in the late 1930s by Mrs Strutt of Down House.

*The Village, Eype* Published by Frith's no. EPE 12. Postmarked 1956 (full date unclear) and sent to Aberdeen. The major change is the telegraph poles. Electricity came to Eype in 1938.

*Eype, Bridport* Published in the Arco Series. Postmarked 3 September 1923 and sent to Staffordshire, with the message: 'Dear Dick, Have just been watching a Dutch boat come in with wood.' At this point, West Bay harbour was still very busy, with a flourishing trade in imported timber.

*Eype Bridport* Published in the West Dorset Series, no. 368. Postmarked 24 April 1935. Another example of this card, postmarked 1938, has a cross in the field above Vine Cottage marking the spot of a Girl Guide camp.

*The Post Office Eype* Published by Chapman & Sons, Dawlish, no. 24379. Postmarked 5 July 1969. The post office sign can be seen outside Journey's End. The post office, at this point run by Mrs Marsden, had a number of locations. It started in 1939 in Wayside House, behind the pub. During the Second World War it was in Rose Cottage, and then moved to Journey's End. When Mrs Marsden moved to Lea Cottage she took it with her. It then returned to Wayside House and the Bartlett family. In the 1990s it was run by Ann Harris at Ship's Lights, and then the final location was at the New Inn, where it closed in 1998.

*Duck's Bottom, Eype* Published by Chapman & Sons, Dawlish, no. 24384. Postmarked 31 July 1962. The house known as Duck's Bottom was originally called Eype Cottage.

*Untitled* Published by Frith's. Unused, 1930s. This general view of Lower Eype was taken from the field opposite the church. In the foreground is Lower Eype Farm with two fine ricks clearly visible. The farm buildings have now been converted into dwellings.

*Eype* Published by Potts. Unused, 1920. This wooden bungalow, built in about 1917, and originally known as Seaview, was erected by a farmer from Watton whose house had burnt down. It was approached via some steps leading from April Cottage, in the main street, the house on the far left of the card. Later it was called The Ark. Subsequently it was replaced by a new bungalow, Yenworthy.

*Eype, Bridport* Published by Hine Bros, Bridport. Postmarked 17 August 1906. This is an early version of the much repeated view up the main street, looking towards the New Inn. On the right, behind the tree, is the cracked end wall of April Cottage, one of the oldest buildings in the village. One night, this wall collapsed, revealing to the world the owner in bed. It was rebuilt with a window.

*Eype* Published by Potts. Unused, 1920s. The post in the right foreground used to carry an oil-fired street light. An iron frame that carried another one can still be seen on the corner of Sunset Cottage, the furthest away of the terrace on the left.

*Eype* Published by Claud Hider, no. 337. Postmarked 24 May 1929 and sent to Upper Norwood, London. This shows the new end wall to April Cottage, with its window, and on the left Tom Forsey's boatbuilding shed. Mr Forsey's boats, hand-built entirely along traditional lines, were known to be among the best on the South coast. At one time the Warren family owned six, used for lobster fishing. Also visible on the left is Beehive Cottage, an annexe built in the garden of Honeysuckle Cottage. The cart, loaded with sand from the beach, belonged to Charles Warren's brother, Rob.

*Eype Village* Published by Chapman & Sons, Dawlish, no. 24382. Postmarked 19 April 1956 and sent to Ringwood, Hampshire. Noticeable now are the electricity poles, installed in 1938.

*Eype Village* Publisher unknown. A similar card was issued by Valentine's. Unused, 1940s. At this point there was a small shop and post office in Wayside House, just visible, and in front of it, in the pub yard, a garage. To the right is a pre-fab bungalow, a temporary replacement for the old cottage that stood on the site.

*Untitled* Published by Frith's, no.E54053. Unused, 1950s. This is the view down hill from the New Inn. On the left is the old school room, built in 1859 as a Dame School run originally by Mrs Ada Silk. In July 1882 there were thirteen pupils, and a similar number in October 1883. By July 1885 there were fourteen, with some pupils absent. By July 1890 there were only five, and at some point in the 1890s the school was closed. On 26 October 1904, thanks to the generosity of Miss James, the building was reopened as a Reading Room for the village, when some 130 people enjoyed 'an excellent musical programme.' Various uses for the building were found in the following decades, including chicken rearing, until in 2000 it was restored and enlarged to serve as a Village Hall.

*The Inn, Eype* Published by Chapman & Sons, Dawlish. Unused, 1950s. Still standing is the stone-built garage in front of the pub, later demolished to form the car park. Also visible is the highly regarded old inn sign painted by George Biles and changed in the 1960s. The New Inn was built as a house in 1837, originally called Paradise Cottage.

*Eype* Published by Judge's Ltd, no. 29003. Stamped but unposted, 1960s. This shows the New Inn, with its recently constructed carpark and, on the right, the former school room. Visible on the far left, on Sunset Cottage, is the old iron lamp bracket.

*Eype Village nr Bridport* Publisher unknown. Postmarked 1905. This is the earliest of a group of cards showing this view. Taken in about 1902, this shows the tumbledown state of the cottage on the left. This collapsed later and was replaced by a pre-fab bungalow, in turn replaced by a new bungalow in 1973, built further back from the street. At the bottom of the hill is Tom Fursey's boat shed, with timbers cut for boatbuilding leaning against it.

*Cottages at Eype* Published by Valentine's. Postmarked 23 December 1903. Many other examples are known, including one postmarked 1927, showing the lasting popularity of this image. This famous view, one of the most appealing of all Eype postcards, curiously shows the cottage on the left in much better condition than the previous example and must be taken from an earlier photograph. The man in the doorway is William Harvey and the girl on the steps is Florence Buttall. Her mother, Mary, is standing further down the street.

*Eype Village* Published by W. & E. Frost, Bridport. Postmarked 23 July 1906. Monochrome and hand-coloured versions were issued, but only the coloured ones seem to have the Frost imprint. Another famous Eype card, this shows Will Gape delivering coal. Gape had a coal, sand and gravel business in West Bay, with supplies brought in by ship and train. Later, he started the first caravan park at West Bay.

*Eype Church* Publisher unknown. Postmarked 21 July 1906. The church of St Peter, ambitiously large for so small a village, was built in 1865 following the gift to the parish of a sizeable private donation. The architect was Talbot Bury, and the pulpit and font were carved by R L Boulton. In effect a chapel, St Peter's has always been a subsidiary of St John the Baptist, Symondsbury. The roof of the rather eccentric porch was destroyed by gales in about 1929.

*Untitled* Published by Frith's, no. E54002. Unused, late 1950s. This shows the Edgecliff Caravan Park and Campsite in its very early days, so named because some of the caravans were literally, on the cliff edge. Owned during the war by Mrs Crapper, it was later sold to Mr Wiffin. Now known as Highlands End Holiday Park, this well-known and well-equipped site is one of the many reasons for Eype's continuing attraction to visitors.

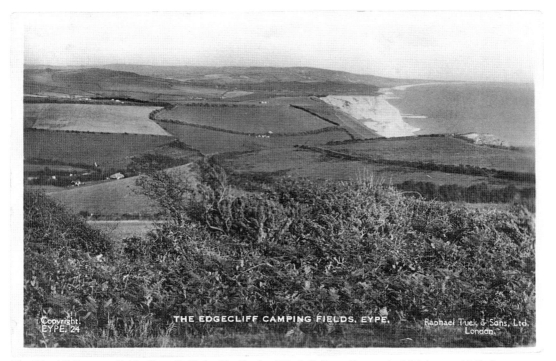

*The Edgecliff Camping Fields, Eype*. Published by Raphael Tuck & Sons. Postmarked 27 August 1949. Sent to South London, with the message: "Its very nice here and caravan is well fitted. Managing very well for food without much cooking. Bye for now".

VIEW FROM ORCHARD, DOWN HOUSE, EYPE, BRIDPORT

*View from Orchard, Down House, Eype, Bridport* Publisher unknown. Unused, 1920s. Down House, an elegant eighteenth century building and the grandest in the village, stands at the highest point in Higher Eype, with magnificent views out over the downs and the cliffs. Between the wars it was owned by Miss Emily Strutt, whose land stretched from Down House to the cliff edge. A noted socialite, Miss Strutt brought many famous literary, theatrical, artistic and sporting personalities to Eype.

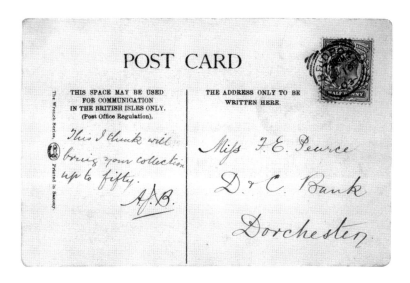

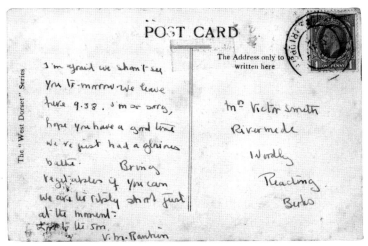

The primary concern of the postcard collector is, naturally, the image, and so little attention is generally paid to the message on the back. In most cases, these are predictably mundane, and reveal how little the technique of postcard writing has changed over the last century. However, there are always exceptions that give insights into the social life and customs of the period, or into the history of the postcard and the postal services. Two such examples are shown here.

The first card, sent in 1903 to Dorchester, has the message: 'This I think will bring your collection up to fifty.' From its inception in Britain in 1894, the picture postcard has always appealed to collectors, a phenomenon that explains why so many cards that survive today are unused. The lady in Dorchester probably put her cards, used and unused, straight into an album, ensuring their survival in good condition for future generations of collectors. Also unusual on this card is the archaic spelling of the word Miss.

The second card, with an illegible postmark, was sent to Reading in 1918 or later (the inland picture postcard postage rate was increased from 1/2d to 1d on 3rd June 1918), and has a longer message: 'I'm afraid we shan't see you tomorrow. We leave here 9.38. I'm so sorry, hope you have a good time, we've just had a glorious bathe. Bring vegetables if you can we are terribly short just at the moment. Love to the son.' This reveals a number of things. First, it shows that the postal service was completely reliable. The Rankins were certain their friends in Reading would get the message before they left for Dorset the next day. Second, it indicates the dependable and extensive nature of the railway network, still for most people the only means of transport. The 9.38 departure from West Bay, the end of the Bridport branch line from Maiden Newton, connected with Great Western Railway services on the Weymouth to Bristol line, and thus with the rest of the huge GWR network. Third, it suggests that vegetables were in shorter supply in the villages of West Dorset than in the big towns, an indication that the card may have been sent around the end of the First World War, when food shortages were still a major problem in many parts of Britain.

The appeal of the postcard has always been obvious. They were a sensation when they first appeared at the end of the nineteenth century, and their lasting popularity explains why so many people today still send postcards, and collect the cards from the past. Various experts and authorities have attempted to calculate, from postal records, the number of cards sent, and the quantities revealed are simply stratospheric. In Britain, for example, records reveal that between 1895 and 1915 around 20,000 million cards were sent. If the postage figures for the same period for other major postcard-producing countries are added, the total comes to something like 140,000 million. These figures do not include all the cards that were bought as souvenirs and never used, another massive, but completely incalculable, total. Even if the survival rate is only one per cent, that still produces a huge number of cards for modern collectors to pursue.

# An Eype Footnote

A family group outside the Sevelons chalet on Eype cliffs, soon after it was built by the Whetham family in about 1911. *Private Collection.* This is typical of the many photographs, and family stories and personal memeories that have been sent to the Eype Historical Group since the publication of A *Peep at Eype* in 2002.